May I Quote You, General Chamberlain?

Other volumes in the
The May I Quote You, General . . . ? series

MAY I QUOTE YOU, GENERAL CHAMBERLAIN?

Observations and Utterances of the North's Great Generals

Edited by Randall Bedwell

CUMBERLAND HOUSE
NASHVILLE, TENNESSEE

Published by Cumberland House Publishing, Inc., 341 Harding Industrial Drive, Nashville, Tennessee 37211.

Managing Editor: Hollis Dodge

Senior Editor: Jimmy Vaden

Contributing Editors: Robert Kerr, Palmer Jones

Research Associate: Jim Fox

Typography: BookSetters

Text design: BookSetters

Cover design: Patterson Graham Design Group

Library of Congress Cataloging-In-Publication Data

May I quote you, General Chamberlain? : observations and utterances from the North's greatest generals / edited by Randall Bedwell.

    p. cm. — (May I quote you, General? series)

    ISBN 1-888952-96-2 (pbk. : alk, paper)

    1. Chamberlain, Joshua Lawrence, 1828-1914—Quotations. 2. United States—History—Civil War, 1861-1865—Quotations, maxims, etc. 3. Quotations, American, I. Bedwell, Randall.

E467.1.C47M39 1998

973.7'441—dc21   98-48025

                                                     CIP

Printed in the United States of America

1 2 3 4 5 6 7 8—02 01 00 99 98

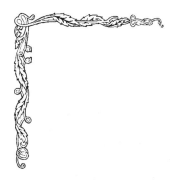

To John Riley Bedwell

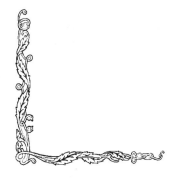
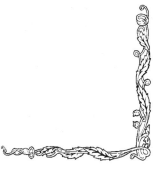

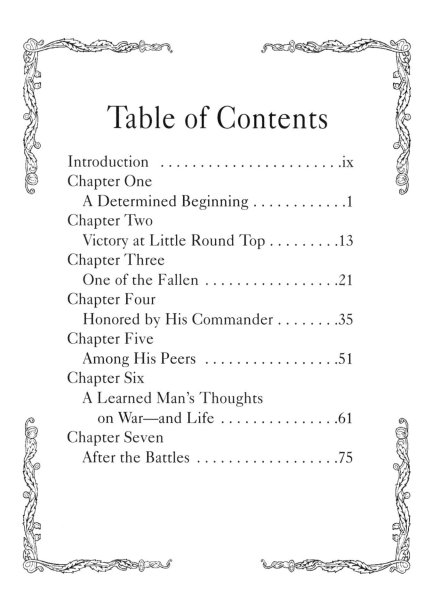

Table of Contents

Introduction

Intelligence, high motivation, and commitment to serve his country were the qualities that made Joshua L. Chamberlain a model citizen-soldier. Very few leaders in the Civil War were as well educated as this officer from Maine. Chamberlain held master's and seminary degrees, and taught theology, logic, and modern languages (with proficiency in seven) at Bowdoin College. He, however, could not sit by passively as the war began unfolding, so he volunteered to fight to save the Union. Although lacking military experience, Chamberlain, during the course of his service in wartime, rose from lieutenant colonel to major general, despite receiving life-threatening wounds six times during battles.

Chamberlain first commanded the 20th Maine Volunteer Infantry Regiment. He gained the honor and respect of his men because of his mutual respect for them, as he gallantly and courageously led them through minor skirmishes and then into the fighting near Fredericksburg. This bloody assault was the demise of many fellow soldiers, whose lifeless bodies took the barrage of bullets to save those still living.

History notes that Chamberlain is most remembered for his military intelligence and tactics at Little Round Top in Gettysburg. Losing and regaining the hill five times, his troops, with ammunition depleted, fought courageously with bayonets to hold the extreme left flank against a fierce Rebel attack. Chamberlain received the prestigious Medal of Honor for his actions during this battle.

General Grant honored Chamberlain by selecting him to receive the weapons and colors of the Confederates at the official laying down of arms at

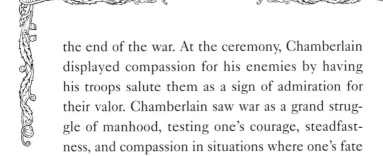

the end of the war. At the ceremony, Chamberlain displayed compassion for his enemies by having his troops salute them as a sign of admiration for their valor. Chamberlain saw war as a grand struggle of manhood, testing one's courage, steadfastness, and compassion in situations where one's fate was completely in the hands of Providence.

After the war, duty to his country remained important to Joshua Chamberlain, as he served as governor of Maine for four successive terms. Throughout the remaining years of his life, he continued to pursue the intellectual activities of writing and lecturing, capitalizing on the intelligence that served him so well in wartime. He never escaped the physical pains of war, however, as his wounds of battle served as constant reminders.

Randall Bedwell
Nashville, Tennessee
December, 1996

Joshua Lawrence Chamberlain

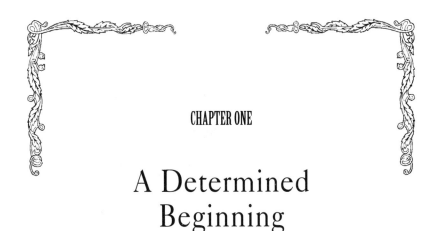

CHAPTER ONE

A Determined Beginning

Joshua Lawrence Chamberlain observed his students at Bowdoin College in Maine as they relinquished their studies to volunteer for the Union army. He, however, was chosen to take a sabbatical in Europe for a year. With a line of ancestors prominent in wars of times past, Chamberlain knew he could not travel to another continent while the destruction of the North was underway. He promptly offered his services to Maine's governor.

Chamberlain received an appointment as lieutenant colonel of the 20th Maine Regiment of

Infantry, comprised of farmers, lumbermen, seamen, storekeepers, and trappers. His high moral character and intelligence were the only qualifications he offered for leadership, but the manner in which he inspired his men became his strength.

After being mustered into the Federal Army of the Potomac, Chamberlain and the 20th Maine fought at the battle of Marye's Heights near Fredericksburg. Bloody assaults pinned them down all night and the following day. Their saving grace was the dead bodies of former friends, which shielded the living from the bullets and ultimately saved their lives. With reverent respect for the role their fellowman performed even after death, Chamberlain and his remaining troops placed the dead soldiers in shallow graves and provided them with a starlit burial after the Confederates withdrew.

I fear this war, so costly of blood and treasure, will not cease until the men of the North are willing to leave good positions, and sacrifice the dearest personal interests to rescue our Country from Desolation. I am sensible that I am proposing personal sacrifices, but I believe this to be my duty, and I know that I can be of service to my Country in this hour of her peril.

—to Israel Washburn, Governor of Maine, July 1862

I hate to see a man always on the spring to get the best of every thing for himself. I prefer to take things as they come, and am as well and comfortable as anybody, and no one is the worse for it.

Have you appointed Chamberlain Colonel of [the] 20th? His old classmates here say you have been deceived: that Chamberlain is nothing at all: that is the universal expression of those who know him.

*—Attorney General Drummond to
Governor Washburn, July 21, 1862*

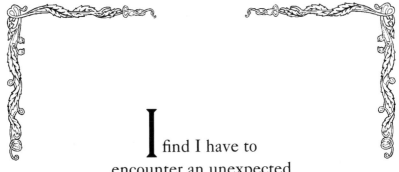

I find I have to
encounter an unexpected
degree of opposition in the faculty
of the College. They are unwilling to give
me any sort of countenance in the matter.
But I feel that I must go, and I trust that
the representations that they propose to
make to induce you to withhold my
commission, will have no more
weight with you than
with me.

—*to Governor Washburn, August 8, 1862*

Does your innocent little head imagine that I could get a photograph (!) taken here? My stars! I fear you have not a high idea of my position. If we can get anything to eat; or anything to sleep on except the open ground; or under, save the sky; if we can see a house that is not riddled with shot and shell, or left tenantless through terror, or if we could get a glimpse of a woman who does not exceed the requirements for sweepers in College, we think we are in Paradise. Why you haven't the least idea of the desolation that has swept through this part of the country.

—to his wife, Fanny, October 10, 1862, near Antietam Ford

I feel that it is a
sacrifice for me to be
here in one sense of the
word; but I do not wish myself
back by any means. I feel
that I am where duty
called me.

—*to his wife, October 26, 1862*

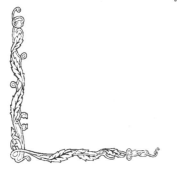

It is cold weather here. The Col. [Ames] and I are crammed into this little tent and at night after dark we became enterprising. We... ripped up a seam in our tent, built a fireplace of stones and mud, topped out the chimney with a flour barrel and stuffed newspapers into the unmanageable gaps, thinking to have comfortable air inside. Since that time we have not been able to see out of our eyes for smoke. . . . [W]e have to stay inside and be smoked or go outside and be soaked. Thus far I have preferred the smoke.

Most likely I shall be hit somehow at sometime, but all my times are in His hand, and I can not die without His appointing.

You need not worry if you hear of a battle, until you know that I was in it; If I am injured, you will hear at once. I expect to get some sort of a scratch when we 'go in', but the chances are it will not be serious if anything.

—letter to Fanny, November 4, 1862

Bless the dear children. I don't dare to think of them too much. It makes me rather sad, and then I do not forget that I am here in the face of death every day. You must not let them dwell too much on me, and keep me too vividly in their affections. If I return they will soon relearn to love me, and if not, so much is spared them.

> *—instructions to his wife concerning Daisy,*
> *their daughter, and Harold Wyllys, their son*

I did sleep, though, strange as you may think it, in the very midst of a heap of dead close beside one dead man, touching him possibly—the living and the dead were alike to me.

> *—Chamberlain's Letterbook, Fredericksburg,*
> *night of December 13, 1862*

We passed some hours in Fredericksburg city. It was a strange sight for this age—so completely battered by shell—from both sides, remember; the inhabitants all gone; the houses, with scarcely an exception, broken open; and everything, left evidently in great haste, perfectly exposed to our whole army. Yet it was far more the effect of the shot than of violent hands, that everything was in such confusion and exposure. I saw no ruthless or malicious destruction. What our men wanted for use and could carry, they took with perfect freedom; but I assure you no mischief was done there under my eye.

—*Chamberlain's Letterbook, December 15, 1862*

Hooker: "You've had a hard chance, Colonel. I
am glad to see you out of it!"

Chamberlain: "It was chance, General; not much
intelligent design there!"

Hooker: "God knows I did not put you in!"

Chamberlain: "That was the trouble, General.
You should have put us in. We were handed
in piecemeal, on toasting-forks."

> *—a heated exchange between Major General
> Joseph Hooker and Lt. Colonel Joshua
> Chamberlain following the disastrous
> battle of Fredericksburg, December 1862*

I never think of this ground but with a shudder .

> *—upon visiting the Fredericksburg
> battlefield after the war*

Abraham Lincoln

CHAPTER TWO

Victory at
Little Round Top

The last of four regiments to be summoned to reinforce Little Round Top at Gettysburg, the 20th Maine received the command to hold the hill at all costs. Climbing up the south slope, the men found what little shelter they could behind the boulders. Chamberlain sent his Company B across the hollow to bolster the left flank. The Confederates immediately pounced upon them. Assuming they were all annihilated, Chamberlain had the remainder of the unit fire on the Alabamians. There was advance and retreat on both sides, as the 20th Maine lost and regained their position five times. When the ammunition ran out, his men advanced with bayonets. Some of the regiment held straight, while others plunged down the hill, much to the surprise of the Confederates, who surrendered or ran. Those who ran were even more surprised when those remaining in Company B, who had taken shelter with the Union sharpshooters, rose and fired at them.

Although Little Round Top was saved, Joshua Chamberlain lost about one-third of his men. He was honored, however, for his courageous leadership in this bloody battle and recognized with the prestigious Congressional Medal of Honor; however, he didn't actually receive it until 1893. His defense of Little Round Top at the Battle of Gettysburg was his most noted achievement during the war.

There has been a big battle, and we had a great many men killed or wounded. We shall try it again soon, and see if we cannot make those rebels behave better, and stop their wicked works in trying to spoil our Country, and making us all so unhappy.

> *—letter to Daisy, his six-year-old daughter, just after the battle of Chancellorsville, May 1863*

Hold that ground at all hazards.

> *—Colonel Strong Vincent to Colonel Joshua Chamberlain, speaking about Little Round Top, just before the battle of Gettysburg, July 2, 1863*

The edge of the fight rolled backward and forward like a wave.

> *—from Chamberlain's official report on the action at Little Round Top*

The heroic energy of my officers could avail us no more. Our gallant line writhed and shrunk before the fire it could not repel. It was too evident that we could maintain the defensive no longer. As a last, desperate resort, I ordered a charge.

Every pioneer and musician who could carry a musket went into the ranks. Even the sick and foot-sore . . . came up as soon as they could find their regiments, and took their places in line of battle, while it was battle indeed. Some prisoners I had under guard, under sentence of court-martial, I was obliged to put into the fight, and they bore their part well, for which I shall recommend a commutation of their sentences.

At times I saw around me more of the enemy than of my own men, gaps opening, swallowing, closing again with sharp, convulsing energy. . . . All around, strange, mingled roar—shouts of defiance, rally, and desperation.

[A Rebel] officer fired his pistol at my head with one hand, while he handed me his sword with the other.

When that mad carnival lulled from some strange instinct in human nature and without any reason in the situation that can be seen—when the battle edges drew asunder, there stood our little line, groups and gaps, notched like sawteeth, but sharp as steel, tempered in infernal heats.

The [Confederate] prisoners were amazed and chagrined to see the smallness of our numbers, for there were only one hundred and ninety-eight men who made this charge and the prisoners admitted that they had a full brigade.

These prisoners of mine were fierce fellows from Texas and Alabama—they said they had never before been stopped.

—letter to his wife, July 17, 1863

There they lay,
side by side, with touch
of elbow still; brave, bronzed
faces where the last thought was
written; manly resolution, heroic
self-giving, divine reconciliation; or
where on some young face the sweet
mother look had come out under
death's soft whisper.

*—on seeing his own men of the 20th Maine laid
out for burial at Gettysburg, July 4, 1863*

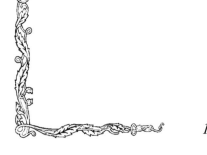

W e are fighting gloriously. Our loss is terrible, but we are beating the Rebels as they were never beaten before. The 20th has immortalized itself.

—to his wife, July 4, 1863

I am receiving all sorts of praise, but bear it meekly.

—Chamberlain, July 4, 1863, Gettysburg

I consider it an officer's first duty to look after the welfare of his men.

—July 21, 1863

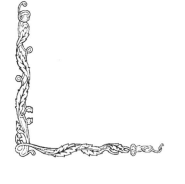

Ulysses S. Grant

CHAPTER THREE

One of the Fallen

In June of 1864, after many other smaller skirmishes, the 5th Corps reorganized, and Joshua Chamberlain became its commander. General Grant's main goal was to take control of Richmond, which would open to them once they captured Petersburg. The 5th Corps was ordered out and then ferried across the James to begin movement toward Petersburg, a Confederate position maintained for its weapons' foundries and railroads.

Although haunted by a premonition of being shot in the abdomen, Chamberlain gallantly led his troops on a bloody march toward Petersburg. Fate, however, took its course. A Confederate soldier fired a shot that ricocheted upward off a rock, striking Chamberlain in his right hip and passing through his lower abdomen. To keep his men from becoming disheartened or placing them in danger by pausing to help him, he quickly jammed his sword into the ground and balanced himself until his men passed.

Grant commented in his memoirs: "Colonel J. L. Chamberlain . . . was wounded on June 18, 1864. He was gallantly leading his brigade at the time, as he had been in the habit of doing in all the engagements in which he had previously been engaged. He had several times been recommended for a brigadier-generalcy for gallant and meritorius conduct. . . . I promoted him on the spot." Despite his doctors' dim view of recovery and the fact that his obituary appeared prematurely in the newspaper,

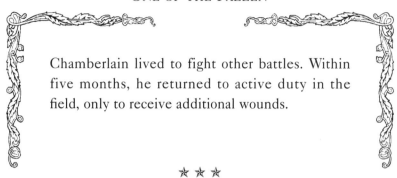

Chamberlain lived to fight other battles. Within five months, he returned to active duty in the field, only to receive additional wounds.

* * *

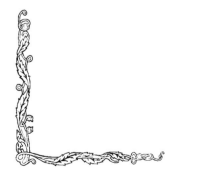

Fully aware of the responsibility I take, I beg to be assured that the order to attack with my single Brigade is with the General's full understanding. . . . From what I can see of the enemy's lines, it is my opinion that if an assault is to be made, it should be by nothing less than the whole army.

—Petersburg, June 18, 1864

We know that some must fall, it may be any of you or I; but I feel that you will all go in manfully and make such a record as will make all our loyal American people forever grateful.

—to his troops, Petersburg, 1864

I am not of Virginia blood; she is of mine.

*—musing on the wound he received at Petersburg
nearly half a century after the incident, and the
fact that he lay and bled on Virginia soil for
almost an hour before receiving treatment*

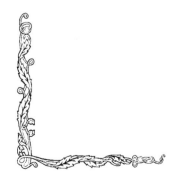
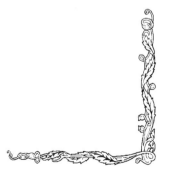

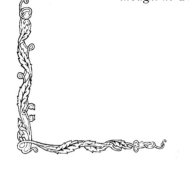

Lay me on one side; I am all right. Go and take care of my dear boys.

—to the surgeon who treated him

I am lying mortally wounded the doctors think, but my mind and heart are at peace. Jesus Christ is my all sufficient savior. I go to him. . . . Do not grieve too much for me. We shall all soon meet. Live for the children.

*—letter to his wife at a time when Chamberlain
thought he would not recover, June 19, 1864*

My recovery is
going on slowly. I am able
to sit up a good part of the day
and am assured that time only
is needed to complete my
restoration to health.

—to Governor Samuel Cony, August 31, 1864

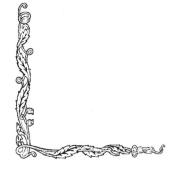

I long to be in the field again doing my part to keep the old flag up, with all its stars.

I believe in a destiny—one, I mean, divinely appointed, and to which we are carried forward by a perfect trust in God. I do this, and I believe in it. I have laid plans in my day, and good ones I thought. But they never succeeded. Something else, better, did, and I could see it as plain as day, that God had done it, and for my own good.

—September 1864

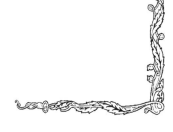

I am willing to fight men in arms, but not babes in arms.

>—*Chamberlain's refusal to pillage the homes of civilians, December 1864*

I shall not feel obliged to lead any more charges, unless it becomes necessary, and hope to escape any further injuries.

>—*to Sarah (Sae), his sister, March 9, 1865*

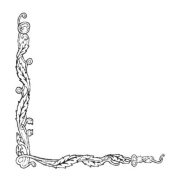

General, you must not leave us. We cannot spare you now.

—General Griffin to Chamberlain when the latter was wounded for the second time, White Oak Road, Petersburg, March 29, 1865

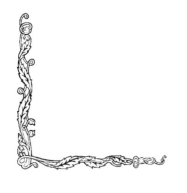

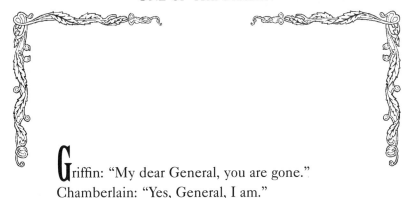

Griffin: "My dear General, you are gone."
Chamberlain: "Yes, General, I am."

> *—After this retort, Chamberlain galloped quickly
> away to rejoin the battle. The feat amazed
> General Griffin, who clearly assumed that
> Chamberlain had been mortally wounded.*

Once more! Try the steel! Hell for ten minutes,
and we are out of it!

> *—the wounded Chamberlain rallies the faltering
> Union troops at Quaker Road, March 29, 1865*

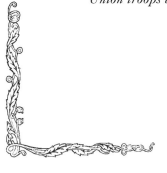

Major Glenn, if you will break that line you shall have a colonel's commission!

> *—challenging his friend and subordinate to assault a stubborn Rebel position at the battle of Five Forks, April 1, 1865*

Major Glenn (mortally wounded): "General, I have carried out your wishes!"

Chamberlain: "*Colonel*," he said, promoting Glenn on the spot, "I will remember my promise; I will remember *you*!"

> *—His order resulting in Glenn's death troubled Chamberlain for the rest of his life.*

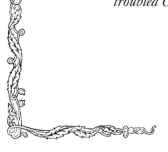

What sharp sense of responsibility for those who have committed to them the issues of life and death! Why should I not have let this onset take its general course and men their natural chances? Why choose out him for his death, and so take on myself the awful decision into what home irreparable loss and measureless desolation should cast their unlifted burden?

—writing about Glenn's death after the war

There was blood at every bridge and ford.

—Chamberlain, commenting on the severe loss
of life in the pursuit of Lee's Army
from Petersburg, April 1865

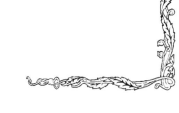

Robert E. Lee

CHAPTER FOUR

Honored by His Commander

Following the Union's seizure of Petersburg and Richmond, General Lee surrendered to General Grant at Appomattox Court House on April 9, 1865. The formal surrender of the Army of Northern Virginia took place three days later, and the honor of receiving the weapons and colors of the Confederacy was bestowed upon Joshua Chamberlain.

His chivalry shone that day as he had his bugler call the signal, and his Union regiments shifted arms from "order arms" to "carry arms." A downtrodden Confederate general Gordon, upon hearing the sound, straightened up in his saddle and returned the salute by dropping the point of his sword to the toe of his boot. He called to his men, who repeated the gesture as they passed. Chamberlain admired the valor of the Confederates as they relinquished their bayonets, stacked their arms, and laid down their cartridge boxes. Chamberlain also remembered the color bearers: "They tenderly fold their flags, battleworn and torn, blood-stained, heart-holding colors, and lay them down; some frenziedly rushing from the ranks, kneeling over them, clinging to them, pressing them to their lips with burning tears."

And as dusk set in, a long row of arms lay before them, evidence of the end of a long internal struggle but offering hope of the dawning of a new united country. Chamberlain reflected: "How could we help falling on our knees, all of us together, and praying God to pity and forgive us all!"

Anonymous Confederate staff officer: "Sir, I am from General Gordon. General Lee desires a cessation of hostilities until he can hear from General Grant as to the proposed surrender."
Chamberlain: "Sir, that matter exceeds my authority. I will send to my superior."

What word is this! so long so dearly fought for, so feverishly dreamed, but ever snatched away, held hidden and aloof; now smiting the senses with a dizzy flash! Surrender!"

—Joshua Chamberlain, on reception of a flag
of truce from Confederate General
John B. Gordon, April 9, 1865

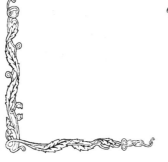

Disquieted, I turned about, and there behind me, riding in between my two lines, appeared a commanding form, superbly mounted, richly accoutered, of imposing bearing, noble countenance, with expression of deep sadness overmastered by deeper strength. It is no other than Robert E. Lee. . . . I sat immovable, with certain awe and admiration.

—*Appomattox, April 9, 1865*

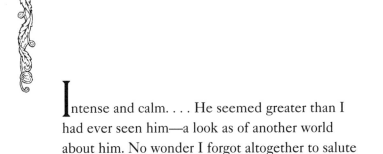

Intense and calm. . . . He seemed greater than I had ever seen him—a look as of another world about him. No wonder I forgot altogether to salute him. Anything like that would have been too little.

—upon seeing Grant after Lee's
surrender, April 9, 1865

Instruments of God's hands, they were now to record his decree!

—on Grant and Lee, April 9, 1865

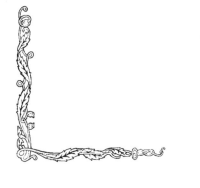

A cruel fate for one so deserving to share his country's joy, and a sad peace-offering for us all.

> *—commenting on the death of Lt. Hiram Clark,*
> *last soldier belonging to the Army of the Potomac*
> *to be killed in action*

Graver destinies were determined on that humble field than on many of classic and poetic fame. And though the issue brought bitterness to some, yet the heart of humanity the world over thrilled at the tidings.

> *—on the surrender of Lee's Army of*
> *Northern Virginia, April 9, 1865*

We were men; and we acted like men, knowing we should suffer for it ourselves. We were too short-rationed also, and had been for days, and must be for days to come. But we forgot Andersonville and Belle Isle that night, and sent over to that starving camp share and share alike for all there.

—on the Army of the Potomac's contributing food rations to the Army of Northern Virginia after the surrender, Appomattox, 1865

This was to be a crowning incident of history, and I thought these veterans deserved this recognition.

—speaking of the soldiers of the 3rd Maine, his old brigade, which Chamberlain requested for duty at the formal laying down of the colors and weapons of the Army of Northern Virginia

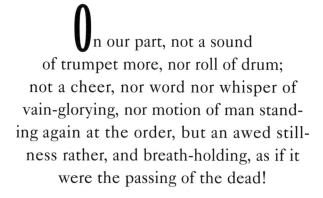

On our part, not a sound
of trumpet more, nor roll of drum;
not a cheer, nor word nor whisper of
vain-glorying, nor motion of man standing again at the order, but an awed still-
ness rather, and breath-holding, as if it
were the passing of the dead!

*—on the formal stacking-of-arms by Confederate
soldiers at Appomattox, 1865*

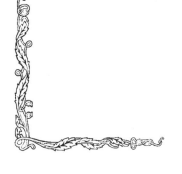

Now the sad, great pageant—Longstreet and his men! What shall we give them for greeting that has not already been spoken in volleys of thunder and written in lines of fire on all the riverbanks of Virginia?

—Chamberlain, Appomattox, 1865

It is by miracles we have lived to see this day . . . any of us standing here.

—Chamberlain, Appomattox, April 12, 1865

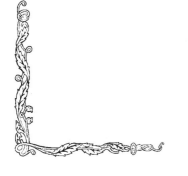

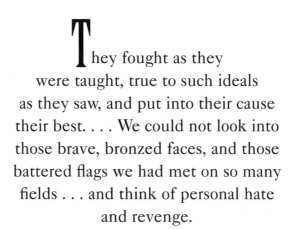

They fought as they were taught, true to such ideals as they saw, and put into their cause their best. . . . We could not look into those brave, bronzed faces, and those battered flags we had met on so many fields . . . and think of personal hate and revenge.

—*Appomattox, 1865*

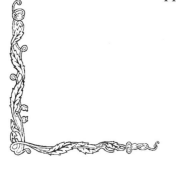

Before us in proud
humiliation stood the embodiment
of manhood: men whom neither toils
and sufferings, not the fact of death, nor
disaster, nor hopelessness could bend from
their resolve; standing before us now, thin,
worn, famished, but erect, and with
eyes looking level into ours, waking
memories that bound us together as no
other bond; was not such manhood to be
welcomed back into a Union so tested
and assured?

—Appomattox, April 12, 1865

Confederate soldier: "Boys, this is not the first time you have seen that flag. I have borne it in the front battle on many a victorious field and I had rather die than surrender it to you."

General Chamberlain: "My brave fellow, I admire your noble spirit, and only regret that I have not the authority to bid you keep your flag and carry it home as a precious heirloom."

—Exchange between Chamberlain and an anonymous Confederate soldier at Appomattox, April 12, 1865

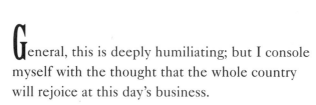

General, this is deeply humiliating; but I console myself with the thought that the whole country will rejoice at this day's business.

—Anonymous Confederate General to Chamberlain, April 12, 1865

You astonish us by your honorable and generous conduct. I fear we should not have done the same by you had the case been reversed.

—Anonymous Confederate General to Chamberlain, April 12, 1865

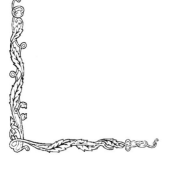

I went into that cause and I meant it. We had our choice of weapons and ground, and we have lost. Now, that is my flag, and I will prove myself as worthy as any of you.

—*Anonymous Confederate General, referring to the Stars and Stripes, to Chamberlain, April 12, 1865*

Brave men may become good friends.

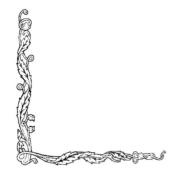

W e formed . . . to face the last line of battle, and receive the last remnant of the arms and colors of that great army which ours had been created to confront for all that death can do for life.

—on the formal stacking-of-arms, April 12, 1865

I t was our glory only that the victory we had won was for country, for the well-being of others, of these men before us as well as for ourselves and ours. Our joy was deep, far, unspoken satisfaction.

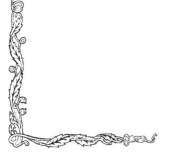

William T. Sherman

CHAPTER FIVE

Among His Peers

His friends in Maine called him "Lawrence," and knew him as a simple but erudite fellow. His wartime companions saw another side of Joshua L. Chamberlain, one of great courage and tactical brilliance. The men under his command held deep respect for him—perhaps because of the unfaltering respect and love he felt for them. When an individual earned some special recognition, Chamberlain, using the eloquence of his pen, requested that the superiors praise them or provide them better assignments.

The officers fighting side by side with Chamberlain in battle relied on his judgment and valued his heroic actions. His scholarly mind and training certainly assisted in his calmness under fire, but his strong faith guided him carefully along the pathway. Union General Griffin, while observing Chamberlain under fire, remarked: "His absolute indifference to danger . . . in the field his mind worked as deliberately and as quietly as it would in his own study."

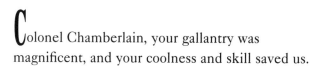

Colonel Chamberlain, your gallantry was magnificent, and your coolness and skill saved us.

> —*Colonel James C. Rice, commanding 44th New York Infantry Regiment, on Chamberlain's conduct at the defense of Little Round Top, July 2, 1863*

I am very proud of the 20th Regiment and its Colonel. . . . The pleasure I felt at the intelligence of your conduct yesterday is some recompense for all that I have suffered. God bless you and the dear old Regiment.

> —*Brigadier General Adelbert Ames, former commander of the 20th Maine, on Chamberlain's performance at Little Round Top*

The conduct of this Regiment at the battle of Gettysburg has rendered, for all time, the prowess of the arms of your State imperishable: conduct which, as an eye-witness, I do not hesitate to say, had its inspiration and great success from the moral power and personal heroism of Colonel Chamberlain.

—Colonel James Rice, speaking of Chamberlain's heroism at Little Round Top

My personal knowledge of this gallant officer's skill and bravery upon the battlefield, his ability in drill and discipline, and his fidelity to duty in camp added to a just admiration for his scholarship, and respect for his Christian character, induces me to ask your influence in his behalf.

—*Colonel James Rice to Senator William Pitt Fessenden of Maine, attempting to have Chamberlain promoted, August 1863*

Colonel Chamberlain is one whose services and sufferings entitle him to the promotion and I am sure his appointment would add to my strength even more than the reinforcement of a thousand men.

—General Gouverneur K. Warren on Chamberlain, attempting to get him promoted to brigadier general, 1864

General, you have the soul of the lion and the heart of the woman.

—General Horatio Sickel to Chamberlain, March 29, 1865

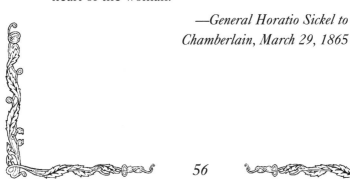

By God, that's what I want to see!
General officers at the front!

*—Philip H. Sheridan speaking of Chamberlain
leading his men into battle, Five Forks,
April 1, 1865*

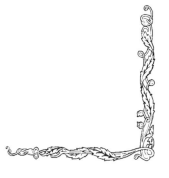

General Chamberlain's bravery and efficiency were such as to entitle him to the highest recommendation.

—General Charles Griffin, April 13, 1865

You have written a deathless page on the records of your country's history, and that your character and your valor have entered into her life for all the future.

—General Griffin to Joshua Chamberlain, May 22, 1865

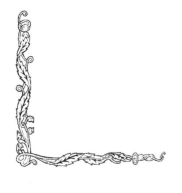

Well, General, honors
have come down upon you
gloriously and I am glad of it.
The way the world reckons it is
a great thing to march up the hill
of honor as fast as you have.

—Reverend Alfred C. Godfrey, former chaplain,
20th Maine, 1866

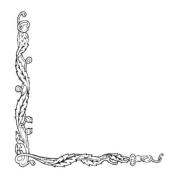

David Glasgow Farragut

CHAPTER SIX

A Learned Man's Thoughts on War— and Life

So dear is liberty," claimed Joshua Chamberlain. This gentle college professor possessed a sense of patriotism so strong that he was willing to abandon a quiet life teaching students theology and logic. Caught between life and death on numerous occasions, Chamberlain watched the demise of many close friends. His gift for the written word allowed him to pen his ideas on the vagaries of war—why such a disaster would take one life and spare another. His words serve as valuable lessons for posterity.

While Confederate soldiers fought to defend land, families, and livelihoods, Union soldiers often battled for mere love of country, patriotism, honor, and manhood. Chamberlain respected both for their ideals and courage.

And in war he saw goodness that might evolve from ugliness rather than just the inevitable desolation. "Fighting and destruction are terrible; but are sometimes agencies of heavenly rather than hellish powers . . . courage, self-command, sacrifice of self for the sake of something held higher . . . fortitude, patience, warmth of comradeship, caring for the wounded and stricken—exhausting and unceasing as that of gentlest womanhood which allies us to the highest personality."

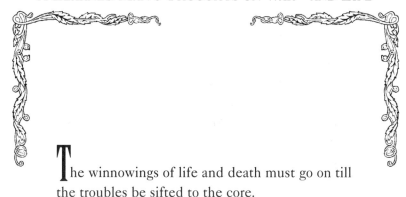

The winnowings of life and death must go on till the troubles be sifted to the core.

It was a remnant of the inherited curse of sin. We had purged it away, with blood offerings.

—writing on why the Civil War had to be fought

Secession must be repudiated with its debts and claims, its spirit and principle. We must have guarantees good and sufficient against any future attempt to destroy this government.

—April 12, 1866

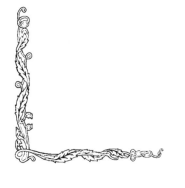

War was no longer a holiday excursion; it was 'hard-shelled' business; not maturing in three months, nor nine, nor twelve, not twenty-four. And the way of it was more bitter than the end.

—*Joshua Chamberlain*

Our place in human brotherhood, our responsibility not only in duty for Country, but as part of its very being, came impressively into view.

—*March, 1865*

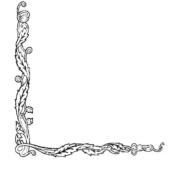

The North was as arbitrary as the South was arrogant. Strong in its conviction of right, proud of its sponsorship for the old flag, the North did not count patience as the chief of virtues.

—1865

Even victory is not for itself, it looks to a cause and an end.

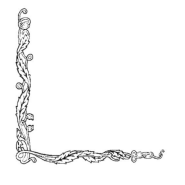
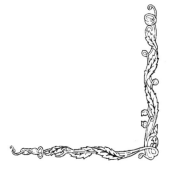

There is no mistake . . . . It has come at last—the supreme hour. No thought of human wants or weakness now: all for the front; all for the flag, for the final stroke to make its meaning real.

We seem the possession of a dream. We are lost in a vision of human tragedy.

War is not a game where there is everything to win and nothing to lose. Those who appeal to the law of force should not complain if its decision is final.

—Governor Joshua Chamberlain, 1867

Who shall tell what is past and what survives? For there are things born but lately in years, which belong to the eternities.

—on the VI Corps passing in review, Washington, D.C., June 8, 1865

Grant was necessary to bring that war to a close . . . we could not call him less than great.

He had a great problem before him, involving issues which the wrestlings of nations and of ages had left unsolved—the confirmation of a new world in its service to mankind and the purposes of God. Grant was a chosen minister of the Divine will, and in a manner was the responsible agent for the execution of the vast design.

What other men could not do, he did.

—Joshua Chamberlain on Grant

In his high characteristics as a man he compelled admiration among these who knew him—even as we did—and he will command it for all the future.

—Joshua Lawrence Chamberlain on Robert E. Lee

What has gone takes something with it, and when this is of the dear, nothing can fill the place. All the changes touched the border of sorrows.

—1865

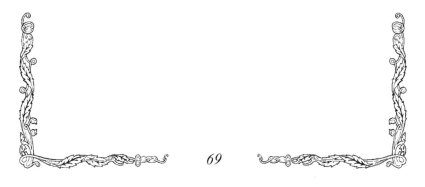

Men are made of mind and soul as well as body. It is not possible to separate . . . courage, fortitude, self-command . . . from other personal activities of perhaps higher range than the physical; because, in truth, these enter largely into the exercise and administration of manhood.

—March, 1865

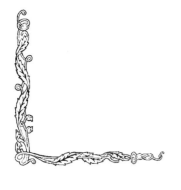

This is the rule and law of manhood: fearlessness in the face of all lesser issues because he has faced the greater commanding one.

Time and tide wait for no man; but man must wait for them.

Sometimes we can do for others what we cannot do for ourselves. And this is the law of richest increase.

Justice is said to be an attribute of the divine: in our imperfect world, missing that, we count one thing noblest—and that is soul.

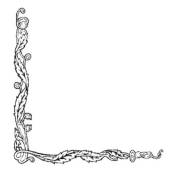

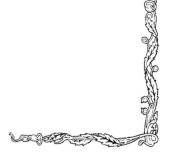

My wish? God in heaven, no more my wish than thine, that this fair body, still part of the unfallen 'good,' should be smitten to the sod, that this spirit born of thine should be quenched by the accursed.

To our common eyes it often seems a dark divinity that rules, and the schoolmaster might interchange the verbs.

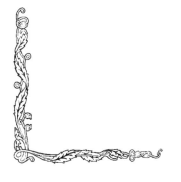
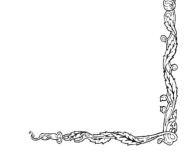

George B. McClellan

CHAPTER SEVEN

After the Battles

That sense of public duty that led Joshua Chamberlain to seek a place in the Civil War procured his destiny once the war ended. After a brief return to Bowdoin College, his popularity as a war hero helped elect him to the governorship of Maine for four successive terms, where he helped to establish the dominance of the Republican party in his home state. Following those years, Chamberlain returned once more to Bowdoin to become its president, a challenge that offered its own battles in peacetime. Accustomed to giving orders and having them followed, Chamberlain encountered resistance from his students as he tried to instill military drill into the Bowdoin curriculum.

Under President Hayes, Chamberlain served as commissioner of education and represented the U.S. in Paris at the Universal Exposition. He later presided as president of three companies and a surveyor of customs. Throughout his private life after the war, he rarely complained about the constant physical pain he endured from his battle wounds, proving that his passion for duty and service took precedence over his person comfort.

★ ★ ★

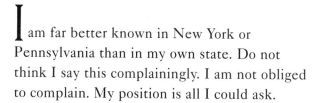

I am far better known in New York or Pennsylvania than in my own state. Do not think I say this complainingly. I am not obliged to complain. My position is all I could ask.

—Chamberlain's last wartime letter
to his sister Sarah (Sae)

You could not say from what world they come, or to what world they go.

—Chamberlain on the Review of the Army of the
Potomac in Washington, D.C., May 23, 1865

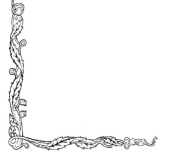

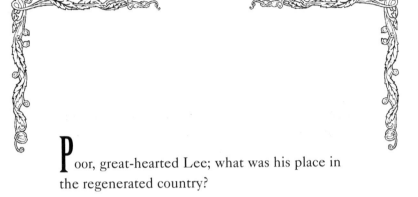

Poor, great-hearted Lee; what was his place in the regenerated country?

We were returning from our part in the redemption of the nation's life—the vindication of its honor and authority . . . what we had lost and what we had won had passes into the nation's peace; our service into her mastery, our worth into her well-being, our life into her life.

—May, 1865

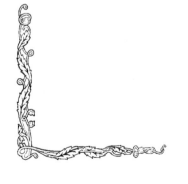

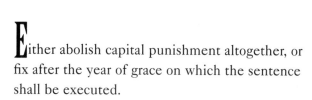

Either abolish capital punishment altogether, or fix after the year of grace on which the sentence shall be executed.

—Governor Joshua L. Chamberlain, 1867

Mercy is indeed a heavenly grace, but it should not be shown in crime. It is the crime and not the man, at which the law strikes.

Laws cannot rightly be comprehended except in the light of principles. . . . Laws show how only certain ends are to be reached; it is by insight into principles that we discover the great, the integral ends.

—Governor Joshua Chamberlain

I know that all true working and real discovery must lie directly in those lines which lead surely to principles, and can rest in no other theory than truth, and no other goal than God.

—Governor Joshua Chamberlain

Hard labor is a prison sentence; skilled labor is the enfranchisement of man.

—November 4, 1876

The college should not be a place where a student can get an education; it should be a light set on a hill, to shine into the dark places below it.

—1878

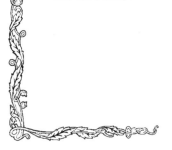

Our personality exists in two identities—the sphere of self, and the sphere of soul. One is circumscribed; the other moving out on boundless trajectories; one is near, and therefore dear; the other far and high, and therefore great. We live in both, but most in the greatest."

> *—Joshua L. Chamberlain, October 3, 1889, at the*
> *dedication of the 20th Maine monument on*
> *Little Round Top, Gettysburg, PA*

We know not of the future and cannot plan for it much, but we may cherish such thought and such ideals, and dream such dreams of lofty purpose. . . . This predestination God has given us in charge.

> *—October 3, 1889*

81

I cannot but think that my day is not yet over for the service of my Country. . . . I desire to be in . . . my right place.

—offering his services in the Spanish-American War, 1898

Great crises in human affairs call out the great in men. But true greatness is not in nor of the single self; it is of that larger personality, that shared and sharing life with others, in which, each giving of his best for their betterment, we are greater than ourselves; and self-surrender for the sake of that great belonging, is the true nobility.

—speaking on the 100th anniversary of the birth of Abraham Lincoln, 1909

I am passing through deep water. . . .
I am trying to get a little closer to God
and to know him better.

—*Joshua Lawrence Chamberlain, nearing his
death in 1914. Infection from the wound he
received at Petersburg finally killed him.*

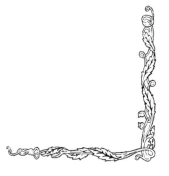